Jaguar XJ-Series

CLASSICS IN COLOUR

Jaguar XJ-Series

COLOUR, DATA AND DETAIL ON
SALOON, COUPÉ, XJS

**Martin Buckley
and James Mann**

Windrow & Greene Automotive

Published in Great Britain by
Windrow & Greene Ltd
5 Gerrard Street
London W1V 7LJ

British Library Cataloguing in Publication Data
Buckley, Martin
    Jaguar XJ series. — (Classics in colour)
    I. Title   II. Mann, James   III. Series
    629.2222

ISBN 1 87200 481 4

Book Design: *ghk* DESIGN, Chiswick, London

Printed in Hong Kong; Bookbuilders Ltd

Contents

Six-litre XJR-S with stiffer
suspension and aerodynamic
additions provided supercar
performance. Behind it is the
Le Mans-winning XJR-12.

Acknowledgements

*Biggest thanks must go to Robert Hughes, the classic Jaguar dealer
specialising in XJ cars, based in Weybridge, Surrey, for supplying so many
of the cars used in this book. Life would have been much more complicated
without him. Thanks also to Peter Frewer, who let us loose with his
beautiful Series I 2.8 for an afternoon; to Robert Smith, for allowing us to
photograph his fine Daimler Coupé; to Derrick and Sheila Thomas, who
gave us time with their concours-winning XJS V12 (finding a mint-condition
early XJS is a difficult job, these days); to Nathan Morgan, who took the
pictures of that particular car, at very short notice; and to Jaguar Cars, for
additional photographs.*

*Martin Buckley & James Mann
London, November 1991*

Introduction

The appearance in October 1968 of the new Jaguar XJ6 made every other luxury saloon look obsolete. Its ride, its silence, its handling were a generation ahead of the competition, even of cars costing two or three times as much. It was beautiful, too, even though there was nothing revolutionary about its rounded form. Familiarity has perhaps made us forget just how balanced the William Lyons shape is, but on considering the car anew one is led to wonder if anyone has built a better-looking four-door saloon since.

Only now are its high standards being clearly beaten — by cars like the Lexus and Mercedes S-Class — and the mere fact that after 23 years it is still a competitor speaks volumes for its all-round ability and appeal. It survives — just — in Series III V12 form, though as these words are being written the end surely can't be far away for this cost-heavy, low-volume machine.

The strange thing about the XJ6 is that very little of it was actually *new* in 1968: it was simply a brilliant reworking of existing Jaguar components in a new bodyshell. Since it was, in fact, intended to replace all Jaguar's saloon cars — an extended family of eight, if you include the Daimler variations and engine options — it was a highly sensible exercise in rationalisation.

With its double-thickness bulkhead to keep out mechanical din, its extensive use of rubber for subframe mountings and specially developed low-profile Dunlop 205 section tyres, its chassis refinement and unitary bodyshell insulation, the XJ6 was a revelation to everyone who drove it. It was in precisely this area that the really intensive development work had been carried out. The rear suspension was not unlike the E-Type/S-Type/Mk X units, with two pairs of coil spring damper units, diff' and inboard discs all contained in a pressed steel bridge-type subframe located on to the shell via Metalastic bushes. At the front, the coil spring/double wishbone units were also subframe mounted in Mk II/S-Type fashion, but with new Adwest rack and pinion power steering and three pot Girling disc brakes.

Although it was always intended that the XJ should have the V12 power unit (hence the spacious engine bay), the engine was far from ready when Jaguar were launching the car. It was decided therefore to go ahead with the 4.2-litre XK twin-cam six as motive power, with the option of a new 2.8-litre variant, both in twin SU form. For the larger unit, Jaguar claimed a very optimistic 245bhp, while the smaller one had an even less believable quoted output of 180bhp. 190 and 150bhp are nearer the truth: Jaguar persisted until the 1970s in quoting gross

Series I XJ12. The sales potential of this short-lived variant was virtually destroyed by the fuel crisis. Few people wanted 11mpg luxury cars, even if they did provide unequalled refinement and 140mph performance. These early short wheelbase cars are rare now. Later Series II cars with injection had far more acceptable fuel consumption.

on-the-bench horsepower to compete with the equally optimistic Americans. Either way, and despite already being 23 years old by then, the XK still felt modern enough and in 4.2-litre guise gave the XJ a good turn of speed with more than 120mph on offer and a 0-60mph time of only 8.5 seconds. The 2.8 was a tardy machine by comparison, though with a noticeably freer-revving feel. It ran more sweetly at high speed and was slightly less thirsty.

The press went into raptures about the handling, ride and refinement of the XJ. It had tremendous cornering poise and was remarkably roll-free for its size. Even on badly surfaced roads it could be driven with precision and vigour, its superbly insulated suspension soaking up bumps with utter disdain. Tyre roar and 'bump-thump' were also wonderfully well suppressed; in this respect, the car was years ahead of the Germans and even the Rolls-Royce Silver Shadow, a larger and more complex car, but from the driver's point of view a far more sedate one.

The 2.8 version was designed as a tax-beater, principally for European markets where cars over 2.8 litres were heavily taxed, but piston problems killed it when the Series II range appeared in 1973. Manual or automatic versions were offered with both engines (the former with or without overdrive), and the cars came with a new interpretation of the traditional Jaguar interior. Leather covered all seat facings, there was wood on the dash, and a fine (if unergonomic) instrument layout with a confusing line-up of dials and rocker switches. All the car really lacked was ample head- and knee-room for rear passengers, a failing rectified in Series II models. Later there were Daimler versions — called Sovereign — but differences were confined to the usual crinkle-cut grille and badging.

If the first XJ6 was a remarkable car, then the XJ12 which appeared four years later was even more so. The flathead, single-cam per bank all-alloy V12 — all 5.3 litres of it — endowed it with near-supercar straightline muscle and with levels of mechanical refinement which no other saloon car could even get close to. Most of the time, one was scarcely aware that the engine was there at all, so silent and vibrationless was its delivery of power. With its four SU carbs, the new unit weighed only 80lbs more than the iron-blocked XK and pumped out a massive 265bhp with 302lb/ft of torque at only 3500rpm. Although it was automatic only — and the Borg-Warner box it used was never really a match for the V12's smoothness — its top speed of 140mph and 0-60mph figure of just 7 seconds are unmatched even by the current S3 V12. A new, simpler grille, V12 badging, bigger vented disc brakes and stiffer front road springs distinguished the new car from its six-cylinder brother.

It came closer to perfection than any other saloon before it, yet it could not have been introduced at a more unfortunate time. Strikes

The XJ Coupé was first shown in 1973, but window sealing problems around the pillarless side windows meant that production was delayed until 1975. It was a slow seller and unprofitable for Jaguar to build. Production ceased in 1977.

hit the Browns Lane works in the month of its announcement, and by the time it was in the showrooms the luxury car market had been crippled by the fuel crisis. The last thing most people wanted was an 11mpg monster like the XJ12, even at the bargain price of £3,725.

Top of the XJ range at £5,363 was the Daimler Double-Six Vanden Plas, with interior trimmed by the Kingsbury-based company plus better-quality paintwork and a vinyl roof. This is now the most collectable of the early series XJs, with the manual change Series I 4.2 saloon a close second.

The Series II range arrived late in 1973, with numerous detail revisions. Early models used the normal-length wheelbase chassis, though later ones had the four-inch longer wheelbase first seen on the late Series I cars. There was new front-end styling with a smaller, squatter grille to accommodate the raised bumper height and revised bulkhead engineering (the double skinning had gone) to make room for the much-improved heating/ventilation/air-conditioning arrangements. Inside, there was a new dashboard with stalk controls rather than the regimented rocker switch line-up and minor as well as major instruments grouped in front of the driver. It was a much more practical arrangement, but nowhere near as handsome. At a stroke, the XJ's interior had lost much of its 'quality' feel, with too many plasticky mouldings for air-vents and the instrument group. Engine power was down, too — emission regulations were starting to bite, and Browns Lane was being more realistic with its bhp figures — so the heavier long wheelbase Series II cars were unable to match the original XJs' top speed or acceleration.

Of greater interest was the two-door XJ Coupé, a pet project of Sir William Lyons, created with North America in mind. It was a handsome pillarless car based on the short wheelbase chassis, with a vinyl roof covering as standard and two large, frameless doors. Problems with window sealing delayed production for two years and the Coupé only lasted until 1977 anyway, with just over 7,000 produced. Most buyers opted for the extra space and practicality of the four-door car, especially as it was cheaper. Today, though it has never achieved definitive classic status, the Coupé is one of the most sought-after XJs of all.

Other Series II developments included new Lucas electronic injection for the V12 engine — bringing big fuel economy benefits — and a new lower-price 3.4-litre car in 1975, with velour seats, to take over the mantle of the 2.8. Later V12 cars also came with better GM-sourced automatic gearboxes.

By now the XJ's keenest rivals, BMW and Mercedes, were starting to catch up. Neither, though, could equal the XJ's still-magnificent chassis, with its mixture of accomplished, wieldy handling and

ultra-refined ride comfort, not to mention the fantastic 12-cylinder engine which even Mercedes acknowledged as the best production car unit in the world.

Despite being past its 30th birthday by the end of the Series II XJ's run, the XK engine was still holding up well, especially with the Bosch/Lucas injection fitted from May '78 onwards to America-bound cars. Horsepower was up from 165 to 176bhp, while fuel consumption was now a much more reasonable 17mpg. The motoring magazines still waxed enthusiastic about the XJ's chassis, though some writers still found its steering too light. Jaguar's reply to this observation was to state that their customers never complained, so that was how it would stay.

In March 1979 the Series III XJ appeared, revealing the most complete reworking of the original car yet. Pininfarina had been brought in to freshen up its looks and had come up with a glassier, squarer-cut roof-line. This was particularly effective at the back, where the slope had been decreased to give the car a more angular look and improve the headroom. There were a host of minor body changes, too: new flush-fitting door handles, big, square-faced rubber bumpers, deletion of the quarter lights at the front, new rear lights and grille made

The Series II saloon was Jaguar's main production offering in the late seventies, Styling became fussier, performance dropped off slightly and quality suffered during these bleak years.

Series III saloon was a final facelift for the XJ introduced in 1979. Pininfarina were hired to sharpen the car's profile, while Jaguar added fuel injection to the six-cylinder XK engine with the option of a five-speed box. The new 'XJ40' replaced it in 1986, but the V12 saloon continues.

cleaner and neater by the use of vertical slats only. It might not have had quite the same classic appeal as the earlier cars, but in many people's eyes it was the best-looking XJ of them all.

Inside there was more equipment: speed wipers, bigger seats (the front seats had adjustable lumbar supports), better carpeting and a tidied-up dashboard.

European cars now had the Lucas/Bosch injection with its 30bhp power-boost (up to 200bhp). This could be mated to the Rover SD1 five-speed gearbox which with its closer ratios aided acceleration and still gave a long-legged 28.5mph per 1000rpm. The V12 engine was unchanged.

The car was enthusiastically received on the whole, though there were still some doubts expressed concerning its quality. This was something which would be tackled vigorously in the years ahead by Jaguar's new boss, John Egan, as part of his successful North American campaign.

The budget 3.4 XJ was rejigged in October 1980 — it now had cloth seats and came with a manual change as standard — while the most exciting news of 1981 was the introduction of the 'May' head on the V12 engine. This more efficient design promoted leaner, cleaner burning of fuel and thus significantly improved consumption.

V12 Jaguar owners could now look forward to the prospect of 20mpg if a light foot was used with the new HE (high efficiency) engine. At the same time, the car was given a more exclusive feel with a chrome waistline moulding, standard alloys and electric sunroof, door mirrors and headlamp wash/wipe. Daimler versions featured electrically adjustable seats, thicker carpets and rear headrests.

The last XJ6 was built in May 1987 as the new 'XJ40' XJ6 began to come properly on stream. The V12 survives it and is built, albeit in very small numbers, on the XJ40 pilot production line. Fine though the new car is, it does not match the beauty of its predecessor. Nor is it as far ahead of the opposition — if ahead of it at all — as was the original 1968 car.

The XJS — Into the 1990s

The Jaguar XJS has led a strange existence. Designed as Jaguar's GT for the seventies and eighties, its outsize 2+2 dimensions and oddball styling earned it a fair share of derision when it first appeared in 1975. In the late seventies, it almost died from lack of attention and sales; but then its fortunes suddenly changed and it became one of Jaguar's most popular cars. In the mid-eighties, there was actually a waiting list for some models and the range has since expanded greatly. There is now an alternative 4.0-litre twin-cam six and a convertible model.

The long-awaited XJS Convertible of 1988 is one of the best-looking XJS models. It came only as a V12 and suffered from slight scuttle shake.

The most controversial aspect of the car was its back end, with those flying buttresses and almost vertical rear window, all introduced in the interests of aerodynamics. From the rear, the car simply looked awkward, especially the droopy light clusters and the stubby cut-off tail. The nose, at least, had an aggressive look and has aged well: even after 16 years, it doesn't appear dated. The impact bumpers were clumsy, though they are much neater on later versions. Structurally, the short wheelbase XJ shell was made shorter still by moving the rear axle and bulkhead forward. The new car shared little with the XJ's interior: there was an all-new and rather tacky wood-free dash and thinner, but leather-clad, seats.

Mechanically the car was an XJ12 but for a rear anti-roll bar, though drivers were pleased to find a manual four-speed gearbox on the options list, the same unit as used in the manual E-Types. Most buyers went for the Borg-Warner box — an ageing unit with no sporting pretensions — but later GM 400s are much preferred. In either form, it was a usefully quicker car than the XJ12 saloon (0-60mph in 6.9 seconds, 153mph in manual form) and it was an unmatched long-distance vehicle, being even more silent and unruffled than the saloon.

Sales were buoyant for a while, but the honeymoon didn't last long. By the end of the decade, Jaguar were in two minds about ditching the car. However, when the May-Head HE versions were launched in 1981 the XJS took on a new lease of life. With its new 'Fireball' combustion chamber design, the V12 suddenly became far more frugal — and saleable. HE cars also had improved cabins (wood

Top of Jaguar's saloon car range in the late eighties was the Series III Daimler Double Six, still one of the world's most refined cars and something of a bargain among luxury saloons.

replacing plastic to please American buyers looking for British tradition) and more leather. Also featured were new-style alloy wheels, twin coachlines and new badging.

The XJS 3.6 was launched in 1983 and was a testbed for the new AJ6 six-cylinder engine, destined to take over from the XK unit as Jaguar's mainstay power plant for the nineties. It came with a five-speed Getrag manual gearbox (the manual V12 car had long since disappeared) and was actually very little slower than the 5.3-litre XJS, though noticeably less smooth. Overall, handling and general response were sharper.

There was also the option of a cabriolet version, with a Targa-style top built-up by Tickford and the rear seats eliminated to make room for the hood. Sales were slow and it was replaced by a proper full convertible XJS in 1988.

In 1991, Jaguar treated the XJS for the first time in its life to a substantial facelift, with slimmer buttresses, new tail-lights and a cleaner but blander look to the entire car. Simultaneously, the 3.6-litre engine was upgraded to four litres.

The future of the XJS lies in the hands of the Ford Motor Company, Jaguar's new American masters. The long-term implications of this situation are impossible even to guess at, but it would seem that the range is safe for at least a few years.

Jaguar announced a revised XJS in 1991 with new side window and rear end styling. In fact most of the body panels were changed. The car benefited from a four-litre version of the AJ6 engine.

Jaguar XJ6/XJ12 Production Chronology

October 1968: Jaguar XJ6 introduced at the Earls Court Motor Show. 2.8 or 4.2-litre engine, manual, manual with overdrive, or three-speed auto.

October 1969: Daimler Sovereign version of XJ6 announced; same car mechanically but with 'crinkle-cut' Daimler grille, different badging.

Early 1970: New Borg-Warner model 12 automatic gearbox replaces aging Type 8 with part-throttle kick-down, better over-ride control.

July 1972: XJ12 Saloon announced. Different grille and badging distinguish the new V12-engined car from the XJ6. Car has vented front disc brakes, limited slip diff' to cope with 140mph performance. Not offered with manual transmission.

September 1972: Top-of-the-range Daimler Double-Six Vanden Plas announced with four-inches longer wheelbase shell and special Vanden Plas trim.

October 1972: Long wheelbase version of other XJs now offered.

September 1973: Series II XJ range announced at the Frankfurt Show. New smaller front grille, higher front bumper, restyled dash, improved heating system. Two-door pillarless XJC Coupé is also announced but does not go into production until 1975 due to development snags. Pollution controls on both XK and V12 engines reduce power. 2.8-litre car discontinued.

April 1975: 3.4-litre Economy XJ introduced with cloth seats as standard.

April 1975: V12-engined cars get Lucas/Bosch electronic fuel injection boosting power from 250 to 285bhp and improving economy.

April 1977: More refined GM 400 Hydramatic replaces Borg-Warner auto box in V12 cars.

November 1977: Coupé production ends.

March 1979: Much improved Series III cars introduced with crisper styling (squarer roof-line, more glass area, more steeply raked screen pillars, new black injection moulding bumpers), fuel injection for the 4.2-litre XK engine and Rover SD1 five-speed gearbox option, plus many minor trim and mechanical changes.

October 1980: Revised spec 3.4XJ introduced. £500 cheaper to compete with Mercedes 280E.

September 1981: HE specification V12 engine introduced with 'May' split-level combustion chambers giving a 25 percent improvement in economy.

October 1982: Daimler name dropped in Europe. Jaguar Sovereign introduced with perforated alloy wheels, improved equipment, but only for the Continent until 1984.

August 1983: Vanden Plas name dropped.

May 1987: XJ6 production ends.

May 1989: V12 continues, can now run on unleaded fuel.

January 1990: ABS brakes now fitted to V12, car continues in production.

Above: The Giugiaro-designed Jaguar Kensington, based on the XJ12, was a conscious attempt to create a MkII-style compact Jaguar for the 1990s. It was displayed at several international motor shows but was not taken up by Jaguar.

Below: Original publicity shot of the rare and highly desirable XJ12 Series I saloon, introduced in 1972.

Peter Frewer's XJ6 2.8 Saloon

Peter Frewer has owned his 2.8-litre XJ from new. Originally bought as a company car when Peter worked as a pilot, it shares a garage with an XJS convertible and has never suffered any of the traditional piston problems associated with the 2.8-litre engine. (Prolonged town use followed by a high-speed run would often result in a holed piston.) The car was built to appeal to buyers in mainland Europe where cars of over 2800cc were heavily taxed, but in fact Jaguar under-estimated the demand generated by the larger 4.2 engine. As a classic buy, the 2.8 makes a good deal of sense nowadays. Its owners tended to be older and more careful drivers, so it is still possible to come across a well looked after example of this unloved variant. By May 1973, when production finally ended, 19,426 had been built, mostly for home consumption.

The earliest Series I XJ is now the most collectable of the breed. With its assertive front grille and abundant chrome trim, its classic appeal is high. It has an aggressive, wide track stance, creating an impression of power. The Series I range was in production from 1968 to 1973 and was sufficiently popular for there to be a black market in nearly-new examples. Body-wise, nothing is carried over from the previous range, although the lineage is obvious. The car was designed to replace the Mk II, S-Type, 420 and Mk X/420G, although the last of these lingered on until 1970.

Has a more aesthetic four-door saloon ever been built? William Lyons' flowing form is a classic of saloon car styling; its superbly thought out wheel-to-body proportions make it look as though it's hugging the road even when at a standstill — it 'sits' beautifully. In general shape, the XJ looks most like the Mk X, especially around the forward-sloping nose and rear of the roofline, but it's a smaller and less corpulent piece of styling. Shaping of the car — mainly using full-size mock-ups in the usual William Lyons style — began in the early sixties and design life was estimated at about seven years. Basic shape, in crisper Series III form, survives to this day.

Above: Mechanically, the car used the familiar XK engine, 20 years old even then (production began in the XK120 in 1948), but well up to the job: smooth, torquey and, with the twin carb set-up, not impossibly thirsty. With its rimmed cam-covers, the XK unit is still one of the most attractive engines around, though few will be found in such beautiful condition as this one. Notice the spacious engine bay — it was built to take the V12 engine, still not ready for production when the XJ was launched at the 1968 Earls Court Show.

Left: Identification on early XJs was sparse: the only way to tell which engine was fitted was by looking at the boot-lid. This car has the rare 2.8-litre unit, of which less than 20,000 were built. Piston problems made it unpopular and although it was sweeter and smoother-revving than the 4.2, there was a noticeable lack of power and torque. Jaguar claimed 180bhp, but 150 was probably nearer the truth.

Right: Only later Series I models had this Jaguar script on the boot-lid. Its makers were so confident about the car's identity that early XJs didn't have the word 'Jaguar' anywhere on the exterior bodywork.

Below: The XJ's boot was long but disappointingly shallow, with the spare wheel under the floor, though at least the lip was low for ease of loading. The tool-kit, as can be seen, was rather on the mean side.

Above: Inside, the XJ's facia kept much of the flavour of previous Jaguars with a walnut veneer dashboard and a fine set of instruments. The major dials — speedo and rev counter — were in front of the driver, with the smaller gauges and rocker switches set into the centre. Efforts were made to improve through-flow ventilation on the XJ (it had been dire on previous Jaguar saloons), but it was still little more than average. Cheaper cars such as Cortinas were better able to keep their occupants cool.

Opposite, above: Centre instrument panel was effective to look at but difficult to use, with a confusing line-up of rocker switches rather than the toggle switches of earlier saloons. A very full set of handsome Smiths instruments covered temperature, fuel, oil pressure and charging, with a clock in the centre. The panel came forward, by unscrewing the retaining screws in the top corners, to reveal wiring, relays and fuses. Earlier cars than this Series I had chrome instrument bezels, but these caused too much reflection.

Right: Seen here is the rare manual gear-shift layout with sturdy chrome-handled lever and switch for Laycock overdrive (optional) in the black plastic knob. Most cars used a Borg-Warner automatic with a centre console-mounted T-handle rather than the old-style column selector which tended to discourage manual use of intermediate gears. Blanking plate with Jaguar emblem hides hole for optional air-conditioning controls. Note period Radiomobile push-button radio.

Left: Vanity mirror in the glovebox-lid was a nice touch, though the box itself offered little stowage space. The XJ was the first Jaguar to offer eyeball ventilation and there was a special Delanair air-conditioning system too, designed to avoid taking up space in the boot as many earlier refrigeration systems did. It was not up to the job of cooling the XJ's interior in really hot climates.

Below: Rear seating in the XJ was adequate, though leg and head-room were thought to be lacking for this class of car. Slim pillars make the cabin light and airy, though, and passengers sat much lower than in previous Jaguar saloons. Those rare standard 2.8s did not have the luxury of rear armrests.

Below: Seats in the XJ were designed in conjunction with Slumberland and had leather on all wearing surfaces. (There was a 'standard' 2.8 XJ with Ambla seats and simplified trim; few were sold.) This Deluxe 2.8 has optional head restraints. Note the courtesy lights in the centre pillar.

Right: New XJ owners got a handbook, a list of dealers and the British Leyland 'Passport To Service'. Since 1967 Jaguar had been a part of BMH and later Leyland, although the effects of the merger had not yet shown any effect on the product.

Below: From 1970 air-ducts were let into the outer headlight peaks for better ventilation. Elegant front-wing shape around the headlights was expensive to produce. The four-headlight system still used a dated foot-operated dip-switch, with a headlamp flash facility on the steering-column stalk.

Above: Special wide section Dunlop E70 VR radials were developed for the XJ — the only car to use them up to the introduction of the Series III car in 1979. They gave superb road-holding, and through clever chassis development did not transmit the high levels of bump-thump usually associated with wide section tyres. Series I cars used steel six-inch wheels with the usual Jaguar chrome hubcaps.

Jaguar XJ6 4.2 Series I

Daimler Sovereign 4.2 Series I

Engine: In-line "six" DOHC
Capacity: 4235cc (92.7x106mm)
Max. power: 245bhp at 5500rpm
Max. torque: 285lb/ft at 3750rpm
Transmission:
Four-speed manual/overdrive; three-speed auto
Suspension, front:
Wishbones, coil springs, anti-roll bar
Suspension, rear:
Lower wishbone, upper driveshaft link, radius arms, twin coil springs
Steering: Power-assisted rack and pinion
Brakes: Discs front, rear
Tyres:
Dunlop E70 VR15 SP Sport on bolt-on pressed steel wheels
Length: 15ft 9.5in
Width: 5ft 9.5in
Height: 4ft 6in
Wheelbase: 9ft 0.75in.
Max. speed:
124mph (120mph auto)
0-60mph: 8.8 secs (10.1 auto)
Overall mpg: 15.3 (15.2 auto)
Production: Jaguar 59,556; Daimler 11,818

Jaguar XJ6 2.8 Series I

Daimler Sovereign 2.8 Series I

As XJ6 4.2 except:
Capacity: 2791cc (83x86mm)
Max. power: 180bhp at 6000rpm
Max. torque: 182lb/ft at 3750rpm
Max. speed:
117mph (113mph auto)
0-60mph: 11 secs (12.6 auto)
Overall mpg: 17 (16 auto)
Production: Jaguar 19,426; Daimler 3,221

Right: The gold Jaguar emblem on the nose was new, and for the first time the front grille was wider than it was tall.

Below: This shot shows the early-type boot emblem, reversing lights and elegant shape of the rear wing around the tail-light, reminiscent of the Bertone-bodied Alfa Romeo 2600 Coupé of the early sixties.

Series I Double-Six Vanden Plas:
The Most Desirable XJ?

This is a rare car. It was built for only one year and was at the top of the XJ range with a new long-wheelbase body shell and specially trimmed interior by the Vanden Plas Coachworks in Kingsbury, London. Only 342 were built. Like the 2.8 XJs, these cars tended to be favoured by older drivers — often company directors and the like — with the result that present-day buyers stand a good chance of finding a well looked after example. This magnificent golden sand low-mileage Vanden Plas belongs to XJ specialist, Robert Hughes.

The Daimler Double-Six Vanden Plas was introduced to the public in September 1972, two months after the introduction of the standard V12. It was the first XJ to get the long wheelbase chassis and was designed to compete directly with the Rolls-Royce Silver Shadow. At £5,363, it was the most expensive car in the Jaguar/Daimler range, though still much cheaper than the Shadow. It was also faster, quieter and handled better, but lost out to the Crewe car in terms of build quality. The basic car was built at Browns Lane before being transported to the Vanden Plas works where an extra three coats of paint were added (it already had its vinyl roof) and the interior was trimmed to a high standard.

Next pages: From the outside you could spot a Vanden Plas by its chrome waist trim and vinyl roof. The extra four inches of wheelbase were added to bring the car into contention with the successful long wheelbase Mercedes of the period. They added 1.5cwt to the XJ's weight and one second to the 0-100mph time. Here it is pictured on the members' banking at Brooklands.

Above: The car featured the usual interpretation of the big XJ grille but with a black plastic V12 badge at the top.

Left: The Vanden Plas name goes back to the beginning of the century and is perhaps mainly remembered for Alvis and Bentley bodywork in the twenties and thirties. By the fifties it was building big limousine bodies for the Austin Princess four-litre and trimming top-of-the-range Austins. In the seventies it built the Daimler DS420 Limousine, although its most mass-marketed products were the 1100 and Allegro Vanden Plas cars. Later VDP cars were trimmed at Browns Lane, and Jaguar stopped using the name in 1984.

Mechanically the Vanden Plas was pure Jaguar V12. The installation was tight and the heat generated was enormous: it got so hot in there that the battery needed its own separate cooling fan. It provided 140mph performance, but following the oil crisis a fuel consumption figure of only 11.4mpg was a definite stumbling-block, for all the car's refinement. With such a good six-cylinder alternative, and given the fact that many Jaguar/Daimler owners didn't actually drive all that quickly, was the V12 really necessary?

Door trims were plusher in the Vanden Plas, with wood inlays at the top and controls for driver's door mirror adjustments. Buyers also gained posher switches for the rear electric window controls. Centre console had gold V12 badge.

Vanden Plas buyers got these thicker and more shapely seats with all contact surfaces trimmed in leather (of course) and standard head restraints.

Rear passengers had individual seats and all had thicker carpeting with thick footwell rugs. There were reading lights in the rear compartment too.

Jaguar XJ12 Series I/Daimler Double-Six Series I

Engine: V12 SOHC

Capacity: 5343cc (90x70mm)

Max. power: 253bhp at 5500rpm

Max. Torque: 302lb/ft at 3500rpm

Transmission: Three-speed auto

Suspension, front:
Wishbones, coil springs, anti-roll bar

Suspension, rear:
Lower wishbones, upper driveshaft link, radius arms,
twin coil springs

Steering: Power-assisted rack and pinion

Brakes: Discs front, rear

Tyres:
Dunlp E70 VR15 SP Sport 6kx15 on bolt-on pressed
steel wheels

Length: 15ft 9.5in (swb); 16ft 2.75in (lwb)

Width: 5ft 9.5in

Height: 4ft 6in

Wheelbase: 9ft 0.75in (swb); 9ft 4.75in (lwb)

Max. speed: 145mph

0-60mph: 7.4 secs

Overall mpg: 11.4

Production:
Jaguar 3,235; Daimler 466; Daimler Vanden Plas 342

Daimler Sovereign Coupé 4.2

Sir William's Favourite

The XJC — or, in this case, Sovereign Coupé — was being hailed as a classic almost before it went out of production in 1977. Built to challenge Germany's BMW CS and Mercedes SLC, it never really caught on in America where buyers expected to pay less, not more, for a two-door car (the XJC was £600-700 dearer than the 4.2 saloon). It suffered from imperfect sealing around the frameless side windows and there were also reports of body-flex. Ultimate version was the injected 5.3 XJC, surely a better-looking car than the ungainly XJS which effectively replaced it? This car belongs to Jaguar Enthusiasts' Club member Robert Smith and is fresh from a home restoration. XJCs are worth more than saloon equivalents (they are much rarer) but if anything are more rust-prone. Certain panels, such as rear wings, can be difficult to find.

The XJ Coupé (or XJC) was announced at the Earls Court Motor Show in 1973 but didn't make it into production until 1975. This is a recently restored Daimler version with the 4.2-litre engine. Mechanically the car was pure Series II XJ Saloon. A pet project of Sir William Lyons, the Coupé offered rather more room and comfort than its rivals, at less cost, but couldn't match its competitors' sales — in particular those of BMW — and was phased out in 1977 to make way for growing saloon production and the XJS. The 5.3-litre V12 car is possibly the most desirable and collectable of the range.

Previous pages: The XJC looks best in side profile. Its lines are pure and beautifully balanced, though the grained vinyl roof is there to hide both the thicker-than-saloon rear pillar and a less well finished-off roof panel. It uses the short wheelbase chassis with four-inch longer doors and no central roof pillar. The side glasses wound down out of sight to give a totally clear side opening. The rear pillar was thicker to meet crash test requirements and the roof was still load-bearing, although there was an additional boxed post behind the door shut face to give extra stiffness. XJ Coupés were 50lbs lighter than saloons.

Above: The rear side windows lowered electrically into the bodywork, tilting forward to miss the wheelarch. Production of the Coupé was delayed because Jaguar had trouble getting a wind-tight seal between the side and door window glasses. They never got it quite right — despite a tensioned pulley set-up which kept the panes under pressure in the up position — but the XJC still had less wind-whistle around the side window joins than any other pillarless coupé. It was doubtless more noticeable in the XJ because of its high standard of refinement in other areas.

Below: The Coupé had frameless doors with simpler trim door panels than saloons. Anything special to the coupé — doors, rear wings, some glass — is growing harder to find.

Jaguar XJC 4.2 & 5.3

Daimler 4.2 & Double-Six Coupé

As Series II Saloons except:

Wheelbase: 9ft 1in

Max. speed: 148mph (V12); 117mph (4.2 auto)

0-60mph: 7.6 secs (V12); 10.6 secs (4.2 auto)

Overall mpg: 11.8 (V12); 17 (4.2 auto)

Production:

Jaguar V12 1,873; Daimler V12 354;

Jaguar 4.2 6,505; Daimler 4.2 1,676

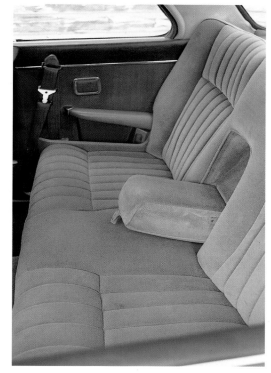

Rear leg-room in the Coupé was the same as in the standard wheelbase saloon (which continued in Series II form for some time) and was fairly generous for this type of car. Inertia rear seat-belts were concealed by the side trim, and unusually this car has the velour trim normally found on the 'poverty' XJ 3.4 introduced in 1975. Rear passengers' power window switches were housed in the centre console.

The Series II XJ was announced at the Frankfurt Show in September 1973 and was designed to answer the criticisms levelled at the previous car. In the process, the car lost some of its classic appeal. Jaguar quality was not at a high point during this period, although for day-to-day driving the Series II was undoubtedly an improvement.

Series II 4.2 Saloon:
Jaguar's Bread and Butter

Whether the Series II XJ is a better-looking car than its predecessor is open to question. Certainly the original feels the better-quality machine, with nicer detailing, though the Series II grille is more well-proportioned. This is one of the most common of the older XJ variants, the four-door saloon with the long wheelbase shell, standardised by the time this car was built in 1977. One could look for a long time before finding an example as pristine as this one supplied by Robert Hughes. It has had just one owner and clocked up 27,000 miles.

Next pages: The side-profile was much the same, though there was now the four-inch longer wheelbase chassis which came as standard with Series II cars. (A standard wheelbase Series II was offered for just one year and is a rare beast.) Extra inches added leg-room but also weight — about 1.5cwt — and during the year's overlap when the two wheelbases were available the longer cars had 'L' added to their designation. This later car has the vented steel disc wheels first seen on the Series I V12 models and an optional chrome sidestrip.

Left: Styling at the back was much as before, except that the number-plate light was now directly above the plate to conform with new regulations. On US-specification cars, bumpers had thick black rubber facings, extra reflectors and repeater flashers on the wings.

Opposite: Most noticeable changes were at the front, where the Series II cars had a new-style bumper mounted 16 inches above the road to comply with American bumper-height laws coming into force in 1974. The over-riders were now under-riders, mounted under the bumper. There was also a big air-intake to complement the smaller and squatter radiator grille, which on V12 models had a black oblong badge at its centre proclaiming the engine configuration. The new side-lights were now under the bumper. Overall, it was fussier than the outgoing car.

Above: The XK engine now had an exhaust-heated air-intake which reduced power to 170bhp — though at least European cars did without Federal specification air injection. Air-cleaner and a Clayton Dewandre single-tube oil-cooler were also new, while emission controls cut the V12 engine's power down to 250bhp. All cars now had vented discs at the front.

Left: Also new was this electric cooling fan on the battery, first seen on the Series I V12.

Left: Power windows were standard on all but the shortlived standard wheelbase cars, with a child cut-out switch to prohibit playful young rear seat passengers. They were operated from this centre console.

Left: Series II dashboard was redesigned with all minor instruments grouped in front of the driver, either side of the speedo and rev counter. Ventilator grille was in the centre of the dash where the bank of rocker switches used to be, their function being transferred to fingertip stalks on the steering-column. The steering wheel had a padded centre to operate the horn, rather than the chrome ring in earlier cars.

Left: Rear seat accommodation was much as before, although the extra four inches of wheelbase did much for rear passengers' comfort on long journeys. Headroom was still limited.

Detail shots on this page show
Series II XJ's new-style door trim
with bigger armrests, power control
windows for rear passengers,
automatic centre console with new
switch gear for fuel tanks (the XJ
had two, one in each rear wing),
map-reading light, heated rear
window and interior lights. Cars
now featured central locking too.

Big changes had been made to the XJ's heating and ventilation system which now featured air-blending rather than a water valve-controlled heater, making adjustments more instant, while the optional air-conditioning unit was improved to give 300 instead of 200 cu ft per minute of cold air. All this entailed a major redesign of the bulkhead.

Jaguar XJ 4.2 Series II

Daimler Sovereign 4.2 Series II

Engine: in-line "six" DOHC
Capacity: 4235cc (92.7x106mm)
Max. Power: 245bhp at 5500rpm
Max. torque: 285lb/ft at 3750rpm
Transmission:
   Four-speed manual overdrive; three-speed auto
Suspension, front:
   Wishbones, coil springs, anti-roll bar
Suspension, rear:
   Lower wishbones, upper driveshaft link,
   radius arms, twin coil springs
Steering: Power assisted rack and pinion
Brakes: Discs front, rear
Tyres:
   Dunlop E70 VR15 SP Sport on bolt-on pressed
   steel wheels
Length: 16ft 2.75in
Width: 5ft 9.5in
Height: 4ft 6in
Wheelbase: 9ft 4.75in
Max. speed: 117mph (auto)
0-60mph: 10.6 secs (auto)
Overall mpg: 15
Production:
   Jaguar 63,282; Daimler 2,431

Jaguar XJ 3.4

Daimler Sovereign 3.4

   As XJ 4.2 except:
Capacity: 3442cc (83x106mm)
Max. power: 161bhp at 5000rpm
Max. torque: 189lb/ft at 3500rpm
Max. speed: 117mph (115mph auto)
Overall mpg: 16
Production:
   Jaguar 6,490; Daimler 2,347

There was a Daimler Sovereign version of the new cars, of course, with usual crinkly grille, number-plate housing/boot handle and Daimler badge on the cam covers. Otherwise it was the same car.

The Series III XJ was introduced in March 1979, a gap-filler before the XJ40 arrived. In the end it served eight years in six-cylinder XK-engined form and it survives to this day as a low-volume range-topper with the 5.3-litre V12. In appearance, many regard it as superior to its successor. Facelifts rarely improve a car's looks (the Series II XJ is a case in point) but the Series III was in fact a successful tidying up of a ten year-old design. This is a mint 85/86 car with the 4.2-litre engine.

Series III XJ:
The Car That Turned The Tide

Early Series III Jaguars can be dreadful cars. They were built at a time when morale was low and the new paintshop was going through all kinds of teething troubles. This late XJ, though, is a very different car, built at the time of Jaguar's well-publicised resurgence in the American market. Nobody had to make excuses for its build-quality, and it was still competitive despite its aging engine (almost a 40 year-old design when this car was made) and very familiar shape. Not a 'classic' XJ yet, but certainly a car with plenty of character. Pick of the Series III bunch is the fully-equipped Sovereign 4.2 with rare five-speed manual gearbox, or perhaps one of the last V12 saloons that are still listed at time of writing. This is a Robert Hughes-supplied car.

Below: Series III cars also featured
a new flush-fitting door-handle.

Above and previous page: Jaguar
had lost confidence in their styling
ability by the mid-seventies (who
can blame them after the reception
given to the XJS?), so for the first
time an outside consultant —
Pininfarina of Turin — was brought
in to help. The most obvious change
was the higher and squarer roofline,
much appreciated by rear-seat
passengers. The front screen pillars
were given an extra three inches of
rake to emphasise the impression of
sleekness. There was more glass
area now — the roof was actually
more narrow to increase the 'tumble
home' of the side windows — and
on the front door glass frames the
quarter-lights had disappeared.
Front and rear screens were
bonded in to form part of the car's
rigidity, A sun-roof was optional for
the first time and all but the basic
3.4 had tinted glass.

Right: Series III cars had black injection moulding bumpers with a chrome-plated capping, indicators now being recessed into the black moulding and the sidelights incorporated into the outer head-lamps instead of being part of the indicator units.

Below: There was a new grille with vertical slats only, rather like the original Series I XJ12. It had a Jaguar head at the top, gold on black on six-cylinder cars, gold on bronze on the V12. Daimler grilles were much as before.

At the rear there was a restyled tail-lamp incorporating a reversing light, matt black badging (with the XJ6 name making a comeback), a redesigned numberplate housing-cum-boot handle, and high intensity foglights recessed into the bumper bar.

Below: Originally all but the Vanden Plas cars had new steel wheels with stainless steel rims and exposed wheelnuts. However, with the arrival of the Jaguar Sovereign on the home market in 1984 (it was introduced in Europe in 1982 when the Daimler name was dropped), this up-market XJ variation had the new perforated alloy wheels.

Above: The only big mechanical change on the XJ was fuel injection for the 4.2-litre XK engine. This Lucas-Bosch system boosted the car's power to 200bhp at 5000rpm. There was an over-run fuel cut-off and Lucas OPUS electronic ignition. A new type of air-cleaner quietened the engine a little. All this breathed new life into the car's performance: with the optional Rover five-speed gearbox, the Series III 4.2 could accelerate to 60mph in 8.6 seconds (not far behind the V12) and deliver nearly 20mpg under most conditions, though the top gear did not have such a long stride as the overdrive-equipped Series II cars with the four-speed unit.

Inside, the Series III buyer gained
cruise control if he bought an automatic
4.2 or V12 model, while Vanden Plas
owners had the luxury of electric headlamp wash-wipe for the first time;
wipers now had automatic park too.
The general layout of the dash was
much as before, but symbols replaced
words on all controls. The newly
designed seats had adjustable lumbar
support and optional electrical height
adjustment (standard on the top
Vanden Plas). This Sovereign has a
different style centre console with more
wood veneer, a leaping Jaguar badge
(or Daimler motif) and a thicker
steering-wheel. It also has the updated
Borg-Warner 66 automatic transmission (fitted to post-1981 cars) which
placed the detent in the selector
between D and 2 instead of D and N.

Rear seating in Series III was still not as generous as in long wheelbase Mercedes and BMWs, but lacked little in the way of comfort. Connolly leather was still standard and this car has optional rear seat-belts. Power window switches, ventilation outlet and ashtray were still positioned on the centre console. Only Daimler's Vanden Plas cars had individually shaped rear seats, though rear head restraints came as standard on the Jaguar Sovereign. Series IIIs had thicker carpeting.

Sovereigns gained adjustable door-mirrors on Vanden Plas cars and wood veneer inlays in doors.

Jaguar XJ6 4.2 Series III

Daimler Sovereign 4.2 Series III

Engine: In-line "six" DOHC
Capacity: 4235cc (92.7x106mm)
Max. power: 200bhp at 5500rpm
Max. torque: 236lb/ft at 3500rpm
Transmission:
   Five-speed manual; three-speed auto
Suspension, front:
   Wishbones, coil springs, anti-roll bar
Suspension, rear:
   Lower wishbones, upper driveshaft link, radius arms,
   twin coil springs
Steering:
   Power-assisted, rack and pinion
Brakes: Discs front, rear
Tyres:
   Dunlop E70 VR15 SP Sport on bolt-on steel or alloy
   wheels
Length: 16ft 2.75in
Width: 9ft 9.25in
Height: 4ft 6in
Wheelbase: 9ft 4.75in
Max. speed: 131mph (116mph auto)
0-60mph: 8.6 secs (9.6 auto)
Overall mpg: 18.3 (15.7 auto)
Production:
   Jaguar 27,261; Daimler 20,490

Jaguar XJ 5.3 V12 Series III

Daimler Double-Six Series III

   As XJ 4.2 Series III except:
Engine: V12
Capacity: 5343cc
Max. power: 299bhp at 5500rpm
Max. torque: 318 lb/ft at 3000rpm
Max. speed: 142mph
0-60mph: 8.1 secs
Overall mpg: 15.6
Production: Still listed

*The V12 Saloons — Jaguar and Daimler — survive in 1991 built in small
numbers on the XJ40 pilot production line at Browns Lane. Only now are
the standards set by the range 20 years ago being decisively beaten. The
Jaguar is known simply as the V12 Saloon, the Daimler as the Double-Six:
Vanden Plas variations disappeared some time ago. Recent emission
controls have sapped their once fantastic performance, but their refinement
continues to impress.*

The XJ6 introduced in 1986 was a completely new car for Jaguar, though nowhere near as good-looking. It continued the Jaguar tradition of supreme chassis refinement blended with excellent handling and cornering agility, though it was not as far ahead of the opposition as the original XJ6 had been back in 1968. The single-cam XJ 2.9 is already dead, criticised for its lack of performance in much the same way as the old 2.8-litre XJ6. It was replaced in 1991 by the much more satisfactory 3.2-litre version of the twin-cam AJ6 engine. In the same year, the 3.6 XJ was replaced by the new four-litre model.

The First Of The XJS Coupés
Getting Rare

Finding an early XJS in really good condition proved a difficult task. It's easy to forget how old these cars are now, and there are few people taking the trouble to carry out a full-scale restoration. The car shown here, owned by Derrick and Sheila Thomas, had only 10,480 miles on the clock when they acquired it in 1989 and is now enjoying a second life as a regular concours prize-winner, taking five first places since June 1990. The 'leaping cat' mascot was not a standard fitting. It's an automatic, like most of these cars, though a few were built with the four-speed manual change. One of those would be a prize catch today.

The XJS, Jaguar's GT car for the seventies and eighties, was announced in September 1975. It was intended to be a replacement for the E-Type, but ended up as the flagship of Jaguar's range, an even more refined car than the XJ saloon on which it was based. Its styling was evolved by Malcolm Sayer in the late sixties and was certainly the most controversial aspect of a car which couldn't have been launched at a more unfortunate time — the back-end of a fuel crisis when V12-engined supercars were little short of anti-social. Production of the Jaguar V12 saloon was down to a trickle, outsold several times over by the XK-engined models. Many felt that the XJS should have been a smaller, more manageable car.

Next pages: It was from this angle in particular that the styling of the XJS didn't work. The flying buttresses running down from roof to boot level gave the car an unmistakeable side-profile and were said to improve the aerodynamics, but did little for its looks.

Above: The front-end featured
specially designed Cibie headlights. (American-market cars had
a four-lamp system to comply with
federal laws, under which the type
of bulbs used have to be readily
replaceable. Some think they look
better, but the Cibies are far more
powerful.) The bumpers were of
the 5mph impact variety — they
sprung back into shape after
impact over a 30-minute period —
and there was a small spoiler
which reduced front-end lift by 50
percent.

Right: This three-quarter view is
probably the XJS Coupé's most
flattering aspect, even though
some felt it bore too strong a
resemblance to the Camaro. The
car was based on the short wheelbase XJ saloon chassis, but with
the rear suspension moved
forward to give a length of 102
inches. Floorpan was 100lbs
lighter than the XJ saloon's and
the body was more aerodynamic
than Sayer's E-Type.

Right: Sayer was almost certainly influenced by the Ferrari 246 Dino, which used a similar type of flying buttress device to rather better effect.

Left: Fuel cap was located in the nearside 'flying buttress'.

Left, below: Note the matt black finish on the lower edge of the bootlid which was a feature of the early cars.

Far right: Despite the XJS' sportier image, it kept the usual big, plastic wheel. Improved power steering at least gave the car a better high-speed steering feel.

Right: Three-speed automatic was standard on the XJS; on this early car a Borg-Warner model 65, on later ones a smoother and more responsive GM 400. Switch-gear was much the same as the saloon's but the top-of-the-range XJS had air-conditioning as standard.

Below: The standard wheels were the same GKN Kent alloys offered as an option on the V12 saloons. Suspension and brakes were the same as the saloons', apart from altered spring rates.

Below: The interior looked more BMW or Mercedes than tradtional Jaguar. There was no sign of the usual wood on the dashboard or door cappings. The seats were special to the XJS and came with leather as standard.

Jaguar XJS V12

Engine: V12 SOHC
Capacity: 5343cc (90x70mm)
Max. power: 285bhp at 5500rpm
Max. Torque: 294lb/ft at 3500rpm
Transmission:
Four-speed manual; three-speed auto
Suspension, front:
Wishbones, coil springs, anti-roll bar
Suspension, rear:
Lower wishbones, upper driveshaft link, radius arms,
twin coil springs, anti-roll bar
Steering: Power-assisted, rack and pinion
Brakes: Discs front, rear
Tyres: Dunlop E70 VR15 on GKN 15in alloy wheels
Length: 15ft 11.75in
Width: 5ft 10.5in
Height: 4ft 2in
Max. speed: 153mph (142mph auto)
0-60mph: 6.7 secs (7.5 auto)
Overall mpg: 12.8 (14 auto)
Production: Still listed

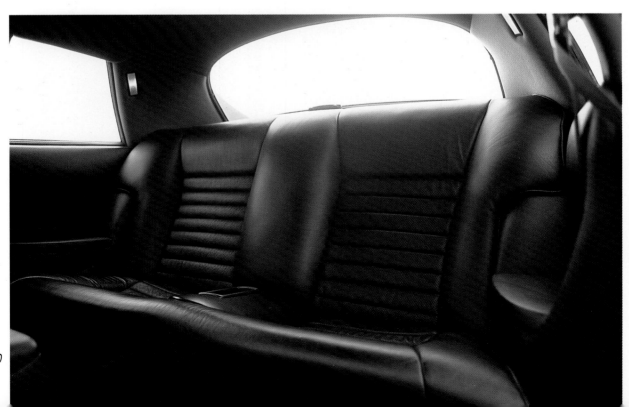

Opposite page, top: On the XJS and Series II saloons the light controls moved from the dashboard to this multi-function switch by the side of the steering column.

Right: XJS owners' manual and service books came in this plastic folder.

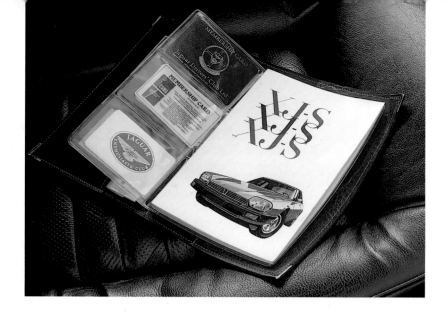

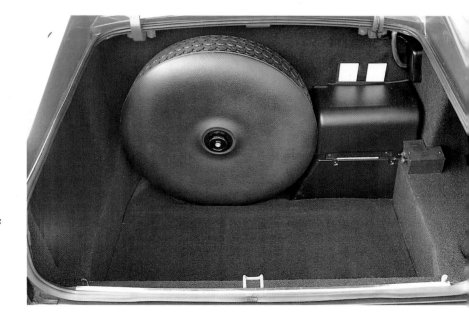

Right: Most people didn't like these Citroen-style rolling barrel minor instruments — they just didn't look very 'Jaguar'.

Right: The boot area was not over-generous for this type of car, with much space taken up by the spare wheel and battery. The fuel tank was carried across the rear suspension rather than having two separate smaller tanks in each rear wing, XJ-style.

Opposite page, bottom: Rear seats couldn't provide the leg-room of the XJC Coupé because of the shorter wheelbase. Small rear window and all-black trim made the rear compartment gloomy.

Left: The engine was exactly the same as in the V12 Series II saloons: a 5343cc 60 degree V12 putting out 285 smooth bhp at 5500rpm. The engine bay was even more well insulated from the passenger compartment than in the saloon: it was designed to reflect noise away from the cabin, though like all the Jaguar V12s it sounded fairly fussy at tickover to people standing at the kerbside. It looks like a servicing nightmare, but most of the essential items are easy enough to get at. If anything, the V12 engine has proved more reliable in service than the XK in-line six, because it is so under-stressed.

Left: Long before Jaguar decided to go ahead with a convertible, Lynx Engineering came up with their own ideas in the late seventies, just to show how good an open XJS could look. The factory car of nearly a decade later dispensed with the quarter-lights and had a neater-folding hood, but was otherwise little different.

Right: Arguably the most elegant XJS of all was the Lynx Eventer of the early eighties. It was expensive, though, and not really much of a load carrier.

Below: The XJS-C 3.6 of 1983 was not a proper convertible, more of a Targa top with two removable roof panels secured on fixed side-rails and a cross-bar, which could be stored in the boot. Because the folded hood took up so much space there were no rear seats in the Cabriolet, just a luggage shelf and a pair of lockers. A V12 version was announed in 1985 but sales were always slow due to the convoluted production process. Somehow the Cabriolet always looked better with its hood up rather than down.

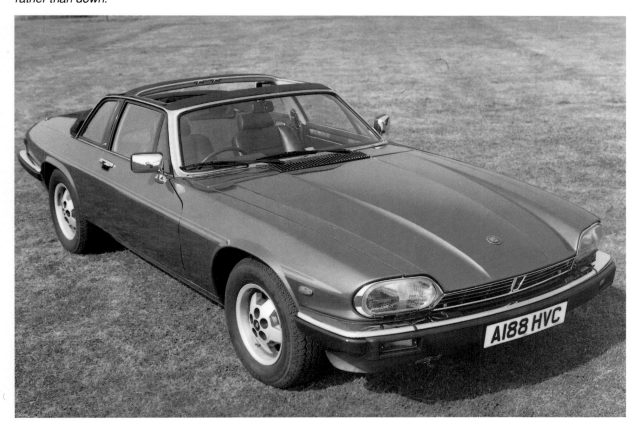

The 3.6 XJS Coupé
Sporting Testbed For a New Engine

Just as they had tried the XK engine in the XK120 before fitting it to the Mk VII Saloon, so Jaguar used the XJS to try out the new AJ6 in a lower-volume car. Good job too: the new unit lacked refinement, though it provided ample performance and was more sparing with fuel. In many ways this is a more sporting car — with the Getrag manual gearbox — than the V12. It continues in production with revised styling and a bigger four-litre engine.

Launched in autumn 1983, the six-cylinder AJ6-engined XJS was the first model to receive Jaguar's new staple production engine, set to take over completely from the XK unit with the appearance of the brand-new XJ40 saloons in 1986. Outwardly, only the badging differed from the V12 HE car. Note the later-style drilled alloy wheels on this 1988 Coupé. Bonnet lump accommodates extra height of new engine.

The main source of interest: Jaguar's new AJ (Advanced Jaguar) 6 engine. It used two chain-driven camshafts and had an alloy block and head which with Lucas/Bosch injection produced 225bhp at 5300rpm and 240lb/ft of torque at 4000rpm. Jaguar also incorporated four-valves-per-cylinder technology for the first time, but in its original form the AJ6 was not well received: it was harsh and noisy when extended, even if the performance it provided (141mph, 0-60mph in 6.7 seconds) was excellent. Subsequently, smoothness was much improved by the introduction of a forged rather than cast crankshaft and modified valve gear. In five-speed manual form (Jaguar fitted a Getrag unit or a four-speed ZF auto), it could accelerate as rapidly as the V12 manual XJS, last built in 1979. Economy was good too: 17-25mpg was possible.
The later post-HE XJS Coupés had new chrome-capped bumpers, wheels and badging, but there were no body panel changes.

This page and opposite, above: Post-HE Coupés also had revised cabins, with walnut on the facia, centre console and door cappings, a leatherbound steering wheel, leather instead of vinyl on the door trim panels and extra equipment such as a courtesy light-delay and a timer-related heated rear window. All this was much appreciated by American buyers who wanted a proper English look to the interior, rather than the sombre black plastic effect of the original cars.

Below: This later 3.6 Coupé has
wool-blend tweed-covered seats.

Jaguar XJS 3.6

As XJS V12 except:

Engine: In-line "six" DOHC
Capacity: 3590cc (91x92mm)
Max. power: 221bhp at 5000rpm
Max. torque: 248lb/ft at 4000rpm
Transmission:
Five-speed manual; four-speed auto
Max. speed: 141mph
0-60mph: 7.4 secs (manual)
Overall mpg: 17.6 (manual)
Production: Still listed

The XJS Coupés and Convertibles were updated again in 1991, with new front- and rear-end styling and a cleaned up side window profile: difficult to decide if it looks better or is a weakening of a highly individual shape which people had begun to warm to after years of controversy. Certainly the six-cylinder car was improved by a more torquey four-litre all-alloy engine. The top-of-the-range V12 XJS featured a new electronic management system and catalyst exhaust system.

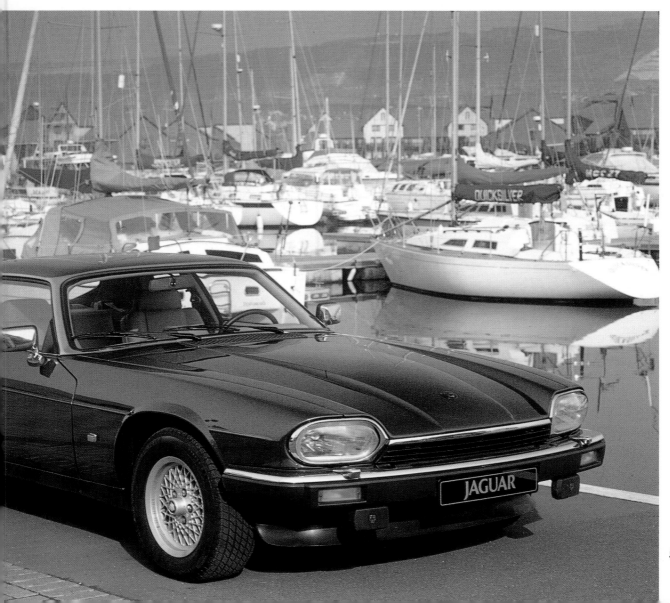

Left: The full convertible XJS was introduced in March 1988. The hood was fully lined and power-operated with a heated glass rear window. The conversion was engineered by Karmann of Osnabruck. Chassis bracing added weight, so perform-ance was down on the standard coupé, but for the first time a factory XJS had truly graceful lines. It continues in revamped 1991 form, shown here with the hood in place.

Right: Coupé and convertible are still in production. Coupé is illustrated here in its 1991 guise.

Postscript: One-of-a-Kind

S taff at H.R. Owen, Park Lane, were understandably perplexed when this 1983 Sebring red Daimler Sovereign 4.2 Auto arrived new at their showroom. Its bright and rare shade of red just 'wasn't Daimler'.

Feeling that there was little chance of selling it to a traditional Daimler owner, they decided to go totally over the top, sending the car to TWR for spoilers, side skirts and BBS wheels to be fitted.

Sold initially for use by an Arab lady, the car was bought by its present owner, Oxfordshire businessman Mark Emery, in March 1985. Its unique appearance turns heads and it once came close to a starring role in the BBC soap, *East Enders*. However, although it spent a day filming, it never actually appeared on the screen. Such is the life of a would-be Thespian!

(Photos Ian Wagstaff)

THE AUTHOR:

Martin Buckley *is a staff writer for* Classic & Sportscar *magazine and a frequent freelance contributor to other leading automotive journals. He has written books on MG, Jaguar and BMW. In the course of his career, he has researched and driven an impressive variety of classic cars — 56 different examples in 1991 alone — including the complete XJ range. Aged 25, he lives in London.*

THE PHOTOGRAPHER:

James Mann *began his career as an assistant to the well-known freelance automotive photographer, Tim Wren. He is now the staff photographer for both* Classic & Sportscar *and its associate magazine,* Your Classic. *28 years old, he lives in London and drives an MG Midget. This is his first book.*